Presented to

_____

On the Occasion of

_____

From

_____

Date

_____

THE LITTLE BOOK OF
GRACE

Compiled by
ANGELA KIESLING

BARBOUR
PUBLISHING, INC.
Uhrichsville, Ohio

THE LITTLE BOOK OF
GRACE

ISBN 1-58660-115-6

All Scripture quotations are taken from the King James Version of the Bible.

Published by Barbour Publishing, Inc., P.O. Box 719, Uhrichsville, Ohio 44683
http://www.barbourbooks.com

Member of the
Evangelical Christian
Publishers Association

Printed in Canada.

Contents

God does not ask us to do the things that are naturally easy for us–He only asks us to do the things that we are perfectly fit to do through His grace, and that is where the cross we must bear will always come.

OSWALD CHAMBERS
My Utmost for His Highest

How happy is he born or taught,
That serveth not another's will;
Whose armour is his honest thought,
And simple truth his utmost skill!

Who God doth late and early pray
More of His grace than gifts to lend;
And entertains the harmless day
With a religious book or friend.

SIR HENRY WOTTON
The Character of a Happy Life

Your growth in grace is not measured
by the fact that you haven't turned back
but that you have an insight and
understanding into where
you are spiritually.

OSWALD CHAMBERS
My Utmost for His Highest

All men who live
with any degree of serenity
live by some assurance
of grace.

REINHOLD NIEBUHR

Lord, it belongs not to my care
Whether I die or live;
To love and serve Thee is my share,
And this Thy grace must give.

WILLIAM BLAKE

All that God has said is plain, satisfactory, and just.
As God in His Word calls us to seek Him,
so He never denied believing prayers,
nor disappointed believing expectations.
He gives grace sufficient
and comfort and satisfaction of soul.

MATTHEW HENRY

God is sufficiently wise and good and powerful
and merciful to turn even the most,
apparently, disastrous events
to the advantage and profit of those
who humbly adore and accept His will
in all that He permits.

JEAN-PIERRE DE CAUSSADE

Grace is the free,
undeserved goodness and favour
of God to mankind.

MATTHEW HENRY

The only reason why any man
ever begins to pray
is because God has put
previous grace in his heart,
which leads him to pray.

CHARLES H. SPURGEON
Sovereign Grace and Man's Responsibility

Never be sad or desponding,
If thou hast faith to believe.
Grace, for the duties before thee,
Ask of thy God and receive.

FANNY CROSBY
"Never Give Up"

For the LORD God is a sun and shield:
the LORD will give grace and glory:
no good thing will he withhold
from them that walk uprightly.

PSALM 84:11

In this awfully stupendous manner,
at which reason stands aghast,
and faith herself is half confounded,
is the grace of God to man at length manifested.

RICHARD HURD
Sermons, Vol. 2

Our work only begins
where God's grace has laid the foundation.
Our work is not to save souls
but to disciple them.
Salvation and sanctification
are the works of God's sovereign grace,
and our work as His disciples
is to disciple others' lives
until they are totally yielded to God.

OSWALD CHAMBERS
My Utmost for His Highest

Grace is indeed needed to turn a man into a saint,
and he who doubts it does not know
what a saint or a man is.

BLAISE PASCAL

But unto every one of us is given
grace according to the measure of
the gift of Christ.

EPHESIANS 4:7

For ye know the grace of our Lord Jesus Christ,
that, though he was rich,
yet for your sakes he became poor,
that ye through his poverty might be rich.

2 CORINTHIANS 8:9

God's grace cannot stand with man's merit.
Grace is no grace
unless it is freely given every way.

MATTHEW HENRY

The LORD is gracious, and full of compassion;
slow to anger, and of great mercy.

PSALM 145:8

Our minds act like a beam of a lighthouse,
picking up one object after another.
God's mind is like the sun,
radiating simultaneously on all things at once.

RICHARD HARRIES
Turning to Prayer

Grace is the good pleasure of God that inclines
Him to bestow benefits on the undeserving.

A.W. TOZER

Grace—getting something from God
that doesn't belong to us.

Our Daily Bread

Go on, dear friends, and may the Lord continue
to bless us in publishing the glad tidings of His grace.
We serve a generous Master,
Who thinks much of our littles.
Oh, that we thought more of Him.

CHARLES H. SPURGEON

Grace, when it comes to us,
is like a firebrand dropped into the sea,
where it would certainly be quenched
were it not of such a miraculous quality
that it baffles the waterfloods
and sets up its reign of fire and light
even in the depths.

CHARLES H. SPURGEON
All of Grace

It is one thing to believe it to be a doctrine of divine revelation, and it is another thing to have the sanctifying grace and power of it in our hearts.

JOHN BLOOMFIELD

Grace is the soul of the gospel;
without it the gospel is dead.
Grace is the music of the gospel;
without it the gospel is silent as to all comfort.

CHARLES H. SPURGEON
The Doctrines of Grace Do Not Lead to Sin

Grace has a strange, subduing power
and leads men to goodness,
drawing them with cords of love.

CHARLES H. SPURGEON
The Doctrines of Grace Do Not Lead to Sin

The grace of God means something like:
Here is your life.
You might never have been,
but you are, because the party
wouldn't have been complete without you.
Here is the world.
Beautiful and terrible things will happen.
Don't be afraid. I am with you.

FREDERICK BUECHNER

Others are as children
playing with little sand heaps on the seashore,
but the believer in free grace
walks among hills and mountains.

CHARLES H. SPURGEON
The Doctrines of Grace Do Not Lead to Sin

Through many dangers, toils and snares,
I have already come;
'Tis grace hath brought me safe thus far,
And grace will lead me home.

JOHN NEWTON
"Amazing Grace"

Now therefore, I pray thee,
if I have found grace in thy sight,
shew me now thy way,
that I may know thee,
that I may find grace in thy sight:
and consider that this nation is thy people.

EXODUS 33:13

And now for a little space
grace hath been shewed from the LORD our God,
to leave us a remnant to escape,
and to give us a nail in his holy place,
that our God may lighten our eyes,
and give us a little reviving in our bondage.

EZRA 9:8

If you wish to know how such things come about,
consult grace, not doctrine;
desire, not understanding;
prayerful groaning, not studious reading;
the Spouse, not the teacher;
God, not man; darkness, not clarity.

ST. BONAVENTURE

Happy are they who know that discipleship
simply means the life which springs from grace
and that grace simply means discipleship.

DIETRICH BONHOEFFER

In all events concerning the church,
past, present, and to come,
we must look to God,
Who has power to do anything for His church,
and grace to do everything that is for her good.

MATTHEW HENRY

It is not a question of praying and asking God
to help you; it is taking the grace of God now.
We tend to make prayer the preparation for our
service, yet it is never that in the Bible. Prayer is
the practice of drawing on the grace of God. . . .
Pray now; draw on the grace of God in your
moment of need.

OSWALD CHAMBERS
My Utmost for His Highest

May God hold you in the palm of His hand.

TRADITIONAL IRISH BLESSING

We may make the Bible a pleasant
companion at any time.
But the Word, without the grace of God,
would not quicken us.

MATTHEW HENRY

The grace of God is,
in my mind, shaped like a key
that comes from time to time
and unlocks the heavy doors.

DONALD SWAN

I must realize that my obedience,
even in the smallest detail of life,
has all of the omnipotent power
of the grace of God behind it.

OSWALD CHAMBERS
My Utmost for His Highest

Those who have lived the most holy and useful lives invariably look to free grace in their final moments.

CHARLES H. SPURGEON
All of Grace

From faith to faith, from grace to grace,
So in Thy strength shall I go on,
Till heaven and earth flee from Thy face,
And glory end what grace begun.

WOLFGANG CHRISTOPH DESSLER
"Into Thy Gracious Hands I Fall"

In rapturous awe on Him to gaze,
Who bought the sight for me;
And shout and wonder at His grace
Through all eternity!

CHARLES WESLEY
"How Happy Every Child of Grace"

But none of these things move me,
neither count I my life dear unto myself,
so that I might finish my course with joy,
and the ministry, which I have received
of the Lord Jesus, to testify the gospel
of the grace of God.

ACTS 20:24

Grace grows better in the winter.

SAMUEL RUTHERFORD

Grace turns lions into lambs,
  wolves into sheep,
  monsters into men,
  and men into angels.

THOMAS CARLYLE

And now, brethren, I commend you to God,
and to the word of his grace,
which is able to build you up,
and to give you an inheritance
among all them which are sanctified.

ACTS 20:32

Every divine promise is built upon four pillars:
God's justice or holiness,
which will not suffer Him to deceive;
His grace or goodness,
which will not suffer Him to forget;
His truth, which will not suffer Him to change;
and His power,
which makes Him able to accomplish.

SALTER

That the name of our Lord Jesus Christ
may be glorified in you, and ye in him,
according to the grace of our God
and the Lord Jesus Christ.

2 THESSALONIANS 1:12

Grace strikes us
when we are in great pain and restlessness.
It strikes us when we walk through the dark valley
of a meaningless and empty life.
It strikes us when we feel that our separation
is deeper than usual.

PAUL TILLICH

Our present enjoyment of God's grace tends to be lessened by the memory of yesterday's sins and blunders. But God is the God of our yesterdays, and He allows the memory of them to turn the past into a ministry of spiritual growth for our future.

OSWALD CHAMBERS
My Utmost for His Highest

Wherefore we receiving a kingdom
which cannot be moved, let us have grace,
whereby we may serve God acceptably
with reverence and godly fear.

HEBREWS 12:28

You can advance farther in grace
in one hour during this time of affliction
than in many days during a time of consolation.

JEAN EUDES

If grace doth not change human nature,
I do not know what grace doth.

JOHN OWEN

Wherefore gird up the loins of your mind,
be sober, and hope to the end for the grace
that is to be brought unto you at the revelation
of Jesus Christ.

1 PETER 1:13

Christianity teaches that salvation is not merely a
posthumous experience, but starts here in this life
on earth; the life of grace is incipient already in our
earthly sojourn; it sprouts here though it blossoms
and fructifies in heaven. The relation between the
"this-worldly life of grace" and "the next-world
life of heaven" is that of the seed and the tree.

JACOB KATTACKAL

There are many among the martyrs
of my age or younger,
and as weak or weaker than I,
but the Divine Grace that
did not fail them will sustain me.

ROBERT SOUTHWELL

If you find God, you find life;
if you miss God you miss
the whole point of living.

KENNETH PILLAR

Our Lord and Savior lifted up His voice
and said with incomparable majesty:
"Let all men know that grace comes after tribulation.
Let them know that without the burden of
afflictions it is impossible to reach the height of grace.
Let them know that the gifts of grace increase
as the struggles increase."

ROSE OF LIMA

Although we may never attain it in this life,
we should desire to recover some degree and likeness
of that dignity (which we lost through Adam's sin), so
that the soul may be re-formed by grace to a shadow
of the image of the Trinity which it once had by nature,
and which it will have fully in heaven.

WALTER HILTON

Let grace come,
and let this world pass away.

The Didache

Apart from that grace,
there was no ability in man to do
that which was good in his own salvation.

CHARLES H. SPURGEON
Expositions of the Doctrines of Grace

But if a man has some good in him,
and if that good could be cherished and be increased and
worked up so as to make men fit for heaven,
what need of the new birth;
what need of the Spirit of all grace
to renew him in the spirit of his mind?

Evan Probert
Human Depravity

All that is good or ever will be good in us
is preceded by the grace of God
and is the effect of a Divine cause within.

CHARLES H. SPURGEON
Sovereign Grace and Man's Responsibility

By the grace of God I ask no man's applause;
I preach the Bible as I find it.

CHARLES H. SPURGEON
Sovereign Grace and Man's Responsibility

He who has most grace
is most conscious of his need of more grace.

CHARLES H. SPURGEON
The Doctrines of Grace Do Not Lead to Sin

Paul assures us that the two principles of grace
and merit can no more mix together
than fire and water.

CHARLES H. SPURGEON
Salvation Altogether by Grace

Arm of God, Thy strength put on;
Bow the heavens, and come down;
All my unbelief o'erthrow;
Lay th' aspiring mountain low;
Conquer Thy worst foe in me;
Get Thyself the victory;
Save the vilest of the race;
Force me to be saved by grace.

CHARLES WESLEY

Surely he scorneth the scorners:
but he giveth grace unto the lowly.

Proverbs 3:34

One of the greatest proofs that you are drawing on the grace of God is that you can be totally humiliated before others without displaying even the slightest trace of anything but His grace.

OSWALD CHAMBERS
My Utmost for His Highest

And he said unto me, My grace is sufficient for thee:
for my strength is made perfect in weakness.
Most gladly therefore will I rather glory in my
infirmities, that the power of Christ
may rest upon me.

2 CORINTHIANS 12:9

I have germs of all possible crimes, or nearly all,
within me. This natural disposition is dangerous
and very painful, but, like every variety of natural
dispositions, it can be put to good purpose if one
knows how to make the right use of it
with the help of grace.

SIMONE WEIL
Waiting on God

Let your speech be alway with grace,
seasoned with salt,
that ye may know how ye ought to answer
every man.

COLOSSIANS 4:6

If the majesty, grace, and power of God
are not being exhibited in us,
God holds us responsible. . . .
Be marked and identified with God's nature,
and His blessing will flow through you all the time.

OSWALD CHAMBERS

But for the grace of God
there goes John Bradford.

JOHN BRADFORD,
ON SEEING SOME CRIMINALS BEING TAKEN TO THE GALLOWS

Grace does not want to be praised,
and vice does not want to be scorned.
In other words, the man who has grace does not
want to be praised and does not go looking for it,
whereas the man who has vices does not want to be
scorned or blamed—and this comes from pride.

GILES OF ASSISI

When I was young, I was sure of everything;
in a few years, having been mistaken a thousand times,
I was not half so sure of most things as I was before;
at present, I am hardly sure of anything
but what God has revealed to me.

JOHN WESLEY

We are not meant to be seen as God's perfect,
bright-shining examples,
but to be seen as the everyday essence
of ordinary lives exhibiting the miracle
of His grace.

OSWALD CHAMBERS
My Utmost for His Highest

Yea, all of you be subject one to another,
and be clothed with humility:
for God resisteth the proud,
and giveth grace to the humble.

1 PETER 5:5

Many Christians are shocked by sin,
but they should be staggered by grace.

Our Daily Bread

If the Spirit of God has ever given you a vision
of what you are apart from the grace of God
(and He will only do this when His Spirit is at
work in you), then you know that in reality
there is no criminal half as bad as you yourself
could be without His grace.

OSWALD CHAMBERS
My Utmost for His Highest

Isn't it odd
that a being like God
Who sees the facade
still loves the clod
He made out of sod?
Now isn't that odd?

Lord, in the strength of grace,
With a glad heart and free,
Myself, my residue of days,
I consecrate to Thee.

CHARLES WESLEY
"Lord, in the Strength of Grace"

The river of Thy grace is flowing free;
We launch upon its depths to sail to Thee.
In the ocean of Thy love we soon shall be;
We are sailing to eternity.

PAUL RADER
"The River of Thy Grace"

Let me among Thy saints be found
Whene'er the archangel's trump shall sound,
To see Thy smiling face;
Then loudest of the crowd I'll sing,
While heavens resounding mansions ring
With shouts of sovereign grace.

COUNTESS OF HUNTINGDON
"When Thou, My Righteous Judge, Shall Come"

Intimacy

Your voice alone, O Lord,
can speak to me of grace;
Your power alone, O Son of God,
can all my sin erase.
No other work but Yours,
no other blood will do;
No strength but that which is divine
can bear me safely through.

HORATIUS BONAR
"Not What My Hands Have Done"

Jesus, united by Thy grace,
And each to each endeared,
With confidence we seek Thy face
And know our prayer is heard.

CHARLES WESLEY
"Jesus, United by Thy Grace"

And the LORD said unto Moses,
I will do this thing also that thou hast spoken:
for thou hast found grace in my sight,
and I know thee by name.

EXODUS 33:17

An outward and visible sign
of an inward and spiritual grace. . .

Book of Common Prayer

Jesus says, "Ye have not chosen me,
but I have chosen you . . ." (John 15:16).
That is the way the grace of God begins.

OSWALD CHAMBERS
My Utmost for His Highest

Grace is but glory begun,
and glory is but grace perfected.

JONATHAN EDWARDS

Let us therefore come boldly unto the throne of grace, that we may obtain mercy, and find grace to help in time of need.

HEBREWS 4:16

If I am not in God's grace,
may God bring me there;
if I am in it, may He keep me there.

JOAN OF ARC

It is all grace.
It is not even that there is a door which
Christ has unbolted, and we, standing outside it,
have to stretch out our hand, lift the latch,
and walk through. We are already inside.

JOHN AUSTIN BAKER

Teaching that lacks grace may enter our ears,
but it never reaches the heart. When the grace
of God really touches our inmost minds so as to
bring understanding, then the word that reaches
our ears can also sink deeply into the heart.

ISIDORE OF SEVILLE

Light us all with your holy grace,
and suffer us never to be separated from you,
O Lord in Trinity, God everlasting.

EDMUND OF ABINGDON

It matters to Him about you.

GEORGE MÜLLER

We'll sing the vast unmeasured grace,
Which, from the days of old,
Did all His chosen sons embrace,
As sheep within the fold.

CHARLES WESLEY
"Hymn 21"

Come, ye who from your hearts believe
That Jesus answers prayer;
Come boldly to a throne of grace,
And claim His promise there,
That, if His love in us abide,
And we in Him are one,
Whatever in His name we ask–
It surely will be done.

FANNY CROSBY
"Come Boldly to the Throne of Grace"

Marvelous, infinite, matchless grace,
Freely bestowed on all who believe!
You that are longing to see His face,
Will you this moment His grace receive?

JULIA HARRIETTE JOHNSTON
"Grace Greater Than Our Sin"

O what a sweet exalted Son
Shall rend the vaulted skies,
When shouting, grace, the blood-wash'd throng
Shall see the Top Stone rise.

CHARLES WESLEY
"Hymn 21"

And the Word was made flesh,
and dwelt among us,
(and we beheld his glory, the glory
as of the only begotten of the Father,)
full of grace and truth.

JOHN 1:14

Cheap grace is grace without discipleship,
grace without the cross,
grace without Jesus Christ,
living and incarnate.

DIETRICH BONHOEFFER

For the law was given by Moses,
but grace and truth came by Jesus Christ.

JOHN 1:17

For if by one man's offence death reigned by one;
much more they which receive abundance of grace
and of the gift of righteousness shall reign
in life by one, Jesus Christ.

ROMANS 5:17

Wide open are Thine arms,
A fallen world to embrace;
To take to love and endless rest
Our whole forsaken race.
Lord, I am sad and poor,
But boundless is Thy grace;
Give me the soul transforming joy
For which I seek Thy face.

BERNARD OF CLAIRVAUX
"Wide Open Are Thy Hands"

I thank my God always on your behalf,
for the grace of God which is given you
by Jesus Christ.

1 CORINTHIANS 1:4

Happiness cannot be traveled to,
owned, earned, worn, or consumed.
Happiness is the spiritual experience
of living every minute
with love, grace, and gratitude.

DENIS WAITLEY

God's grace produces men and women
with a strong family likeness to Jesus Christ.

OSWALD CHAMBERS
My Utmost for His Highest

Costly grace is the treasure hidden in the field;
for the sake of it a man will gladly go and sell
all that he has. It is costly because it costs a man
his life, and it is grace because it gives a man
the only true life.

DIETRICH BONHOEFFER

Those who die in grace
go no further from us than God—
and God is very near.

PIERRE TEILHARD DE CHARDIN

I wasn't christened in a church,
but I was sprinkled from morning to night
with the dew of grace.

RUFUS JONES

Let the word of Christ dwell in you richly
in all wisdom; teaching and admonishing one
another in psalms and hymns and spiritual songs,
singing with grace in your hearts to the Lord.

COLOSSIANS 3:16

Sometimes the grace of God
appears wonderfully in young children.

MATTHEW HENRY

Man may dismiss compassion from his heart,
but God never will.

WILLIAM COWPER

God's richness is such that He can totally give Himself to every man, can be there only for him— and likewise for a second and third, for millions and thousands of millions. That is the mystery of his infinity and inexhaustible richness.

LADISLAUS BOROS
Hidden God

Let grace and goodness be the
principal loadstone of thy affections.
For love, which hath ends, will have an end,
whereas that which is founded on true virtue
will always continue.

JOHN DRYDEN

Therefore, as ye abound in every thing,
in faith, and utterance, and knowledge,
and in all diligence, and in your love to us,
see that ye abound in this grace also.

2 CORINTHIANS 8:7

What is grace?
It is the inspiration from on high;
it is love; it is liberty. Grace is the spirit of law.
This discovery of the spirit of law belongs to Saint Paul,
and what he calls "grace" from a heavenly point of view,
we, from an earthly point, call "righteousness."

VICTOR HUGO

We are here to add to the sum of human goodness—
To prove the thing exists.
And however futile each individual
act of courage or generosity,
self-sacrifice or grace—
it still proves the thing exists.

JOSEPHINE HART

Love that reaches up is adoration.
Love that reaches across is affection.
Love that reaches down is grace.

DONALD GREY BARNHOUSE

May [God] grant you all things which your heart desires, and may [He] give you a husband and a home and gracious concord, for there is nothing greater and better than this—when a husband and wife keep a household in oneness of mind—a great woe to their enemies and joy to their friends—and win high renown.

HOMER

The grace of the Lord Jesus Christ,
and the love of God, and the communion of
the Holy Ghost, be with you all.
Amen.

2 CORINTHIANS 13:14

Our Lord never put His trust in any person.
Yet He was never suspicious, never bitter,
and never lost hope for anyone,
because He put His trust in God first.
He trusted absolutely in what God's grace
could do for others.

OSWALD CHAMBERS
My Utmost for His Highest

Grace is love that cares
and stoops and rescues.

JOHN STOTT

While He made atonement for our transgressions,
He has procured for us the Spirit of all grace
to renew our nature, to transform us into the
likeness of Himself, and to prepare us in the
use of means for the inheritance
of the saints in light.

EVAN PROBERT
Human Depravity

And when I have finished life's voyage at last,
When safe in the harbor my anchor is cast,
The theme of my praises forever shall be,
God's grace, which is always sufficient for me.

LEILA NAYLOR MORRIS
"His Grace Is Sufficient for Me"

May God bestow on us His grace,
With blessings rich provide us,
And may the brightness of His face
To life eternal guide us

MARTIN LUTHER
"May God Bestow on Us His Grace"

So shall they be life unto thy soul,
and grace to thy neck.

PROVERBS 3:22

It's for you I created the universe [says God].
I love you. There's only one catch.
Like any other gift, the gift of grace can be yours
only if you'll reach out and take it.
Maybe being able to reach out and take
it is a gift, too.

FREDERICK BUECHNER

The grace you had yesterday
will not be sufficient for today.
Grace is the overflowing favor of God,
and you can always count on it being
available to draw upon as needed.

OSWALD CHAMBERS
My Utmost for His Highest

And God is able to make all grace
abound toward you; that ye,
always having all sufficiency in all things,
may abound to every good work.

2 CORINTHIANS 9:8

Not what we wish, but what we need,
Oh, let Thy grace supply!

JAMES MERRICK

God ne'er afflicts us more than our desert,
Though He may seem to overact His part;
Sometimes He strikes us more than flesh can bear,
But yet still less than Grace can suffer here.

ROBERT HERRICK

O our God,
let Your grace be sufficient for us.

BENJAMIN JENKS

Even the righteousness of God which is by faith
of Jesus Christ unto all and upon all them that believe:
for there is no difference: For all have sinned, and come
short of the glory of God; being justified freely by his
grace through the redemption that is in Christ Jesus.

ROMANS 3:22-24

God never built a Christian strong enough
to carry today's duties and tomorrow's anxieties
piled on top of them.

THEODORE LEDYARD CUYLER

These things, good Lord,
that we pray for,
give us Thy grace to labour for.

Thomas More

Grace is everything for nothing.
It's helping the helpless, going to those
who cannot come in their own strength.

LEHMAN STRAUSS

We do not need the grace of God to withstand crises—human nature and pride are sufficient for us to face the stress and strain magnificently. But it does require the supernatural grace of God to live twenty-four hours of every day as a saint, going through drudgery and living an ordinary, unnoticed, and ignored existence as a disciple of Jesus.

OSWALD CHAMBERS
My Utmost for His Highest

Salvation by grace can only be
gripped by the hand of faith;
the attempt to lay hold upon it
by the doing of certain acts of law
would cause the grace to evaporate.

CHARLES H. SPURGEON
All of Grace

From first to last, from the "A" to the "Z" of the heavenly alphabet, everything in salvation is of grace and grace alone.

CHARLES H. SPURGEON
The Doctrines of Grace Do Not Lead to Sin

For by grace are ye saved through faith;
and that not of yourselves:
it is the gift of God.

EPHESIANS 2:8

If we can say of any man, or of any set of people, "Ye are saved," we shall have to preface it with the words "by grace." There is no other present salvation except that which begins and ends with grace.

CHARLES H. SPURGEON
All of Grace

New hopes come crowding
on the man who is saved by grace.

CHARLES H. SPURGEON
The Doctrines of Grace Do Not Lead to Sin

Grace first inscribed my name
In God's eternal book;
'Twas grace that gave me to the Lamb,
Who all my sorrows took.

AUGUSTUS M. TOPLADY
"Grace, 'Tis a Charming Sound"

I hear it in the twilight still,
And at the sunset hour–
I'm saved by grace! What words can thrill
With such a magic power?

FANNY CROSBY
"A Message Sweet Is Borne to Me"

I thank the goodness and the grace
Which on my birth have smiled
And made me, in these Christian days,
A happy Christian child.

JANE TAYLOR
"A Child's Hymn of Praise"

There is no such way to attain to a greater measure of grace as for a man to live up to the little grace he has.

PHILLIPS BROOKS

I thank God for my handicaps,
for through them I have found myself,
my work, and my God.

HELEN KELLER

Grace is more than unmerited favor.
If you feed a tramp who calls on you,
that is unmerited favor, but it is scarcely grace.
But suppose that after robbing you,
you then feed him. That would be grace.
Grace, then, is favor shown where there is
positive demerit in the one receiving it.

THOMAS CARLYLE

Clothed in garments of salvation,
At Thy table is our place,
We rejoice, and Thou rejoicest,
In the riches of Thy grace

JAMES GEORGE DECK
"Abba Father! We Approach Thee"

For Thy mercy and Thy grace,
Constant through another year,
Hear our song of thankfulness;
Jesus, our Redeemer, hear.

HENRY DOWNTON
"For Thy Mercy and Thy Grace"